LAUREN GARLAND
Darling

I0191451

BROKEN SLEEP BOOKS

Published 2020,
Broken Sleep Books:
Cornwall / Wales

brokensleepbooks.com

First Edition

Lay out your unrest.

Publisher/Editor: Aaron Kent
Editor: Charlie Baylis

Typeset in UK by Aaron Kent

Broken Sleep Books is committed to
a sustainable future for our planet,
and therefore uses print on
demand publication.

brokensleepbooks@gmail.com

ISBN: 978-1-913642-19-8

Contents

Darling

Lauren Garland

Boy is it good to see you, Alicia

After *The Good Wife*

Tights and those too tight pencil skirts
are tiresome. I can unhook my bra
and wear my grandma's jumper
with its month-old yogurt crust
in the shape of Madagascar
                    and you don't mind.

Aside from the fact that your hair
fits your head exactly
like auburn Lego
the thing I admire about you
is how much you do in an hour –

those daffodils in the office-kitchen
reminded me of you,
furled shyly in buds
when I rolled in at 9,
by lunch half their ranks
had broken into yellow.
That must be a life stage
for a flower, adolescence perhaps,
done with in a morning.
                    And you –

you can wrest the accused
from the prosecutor's clutches
then sit on a bar stool
across from your lover,
fingering a wineglass
while brandishing *that* smile –
did I mention you're a window
flung back on its hinges?

Oh, if you're ever in town
could you hold your heels in your hands,

softly climb the stairs at night,
push the hair back from my face
like you do your darling daughter?

Night in Black and Gold
After James Abbott McNeill Whistler

Tonight I leaned at the office window as slate grey smoke
choked an ash white sky   the fire at the recycling plant

on Frederick Road   it drew me back to this nocturne   the night
in black and gold   those clouds hurling their moods around

like frustrated artists   I swear I see figures in the water
reflected somehow but it doesn't make sense   and a phoenix

or a ghost ship exploding   you reckon they're fireworks
you're probably right   we hover like this by any given

masterpiece   at any tower block window   colouring the world
over half pints of ale   remember our night in the '70s club

the minutes we spent sketching tangerines   I showed you
my scribbles in orange and grey   you taught me to shade

it was cold   still December   we necked Campari   shimmied
round our bar stools to Stevie Wonder   some guy

took our picture   and later   huddled at the bus stop   we burned
through a couple of Marlborough Gold   scorched the black canvas

After a Wedding

We sink into bed in most of our clothes
    you kick off your Docs   it's all you can manage

I lean across   loosen your tie
    quieter here than at home   you say

but the rumble of lorries over the farm
    runs constant as waves   *if we think of the sea*

we can make it the sea I say   as you close
    your eyes   our single beds are drifting

into separate nights   I hook my foot
    around your calf   I swear this room

has started to rise   the floral lampshades
    the minibar   the painting of Penzance

all bob in the dark   I want you to see
    but you've washed up on another shore

left me to lie with the swell of your chest
    pulling in   giving back   then deeper   steadier

Scrambling Eggs

He can't be with you every morning
so he tells you it's time you learn for yourself.
He hangs at your shoulder. You reach for the milk –
no he says, and *remember to whisk*

a breeze through the bowl, it's not a tornado.
So you do, and you warm a pan and watch
a lump of butter foam and dissipate.
More. You do, and you pour in the egg

and nothing much happens to begin with.
You're soft with your spatula – he likes that.
You eye up the salt but *not yet*
so you scrape the sides folding white

into yolk in a figure of eight, then grind.
There, he says, and brushes your wrist
and before you're sure the eggs are cooked
he's killed the flame under the pan.

Tuna

After *Jiro Dreams of Sushi*

This place we live has no rooms
to speak of   it's one great hall of darkness
    the name of a man is uttered on the docks
drawn under by the waves and carried
    on the current   *Jiro*   we feel it swell
in the sea with the tenor of a dream   *Jiro*
    curse or promise we don't know which
it works beneath our gills   we must
    swim through it   brothers and sisters
left and right   our eyes and mouths
    fixed open   *Jiro*   foams
on the tongues of the waves as they lap
    at the boats   *Jiro   Jiro*
Jiro   calling for the nets to be cast

Peeling an Egg

Now and then a bloody fleck
disturbs the white –
a blot of failed liver?
Surely the organs grow
in the serious yellow –
the not-quite gizzard,
the almost gut, the heart
unfulfilled. Strange to cup it
whole and nude in my palm,

to feel something like a god.

Rabbits Hanging Round the Stall

We are skinned,
    we hang by our feet.
Children ask their fathers
    why our eyes bulge out
like someone wrapped
    their hands around our chests
and wrung the breath from us.
    But death is more reserved
than one might think –
    how patient, and tidy,
and distantly unloaded.
    It cuts the air like a swift
then it makes a mild fuss:
    a little round of lead in all of us –
the sweetest, pinkest
    bunting to dress the stall.
Now lay us in your paper bed –
    our flesh is cold.

Waking up with Leonidas

A cat flap goes at the edge of the forest.
I sleep a minute longer then wake

to a shape blundering across the covers.
You're not supposed to be clumsy, Leonidas.

You're not supposed to love me but hey,
cheers for the cold rippling off your coat,

for your belly swinging like a purse full of silver.
I roll onto my back, chest becomes a podium –

you've won again with your meat breath, Leonidas.
With your white-tipped tail curving to a question

& the answer is yes (let me put on my slippers),
the answer will always be yes.

Archivist

He plunders the suburbs for minor tragedies. Smoke stains creeping up the curtain of the end-terrace. Fake geraniums in the window box at News & Booze, a bee's devotion to the plastic stamens. Cracks in the tarmac, swollen with ice. Antique dolls house dumped in a skip. Boarded-up semi and on the pavement outside – a mattress of flattened packing boxes, damp advancing. Black cat curled on a wheelie bin, one eye open a dizzying green. As he reaches for its cheek, it slinks through a break in the fence.

With the tedium of a key in a lock he turns around these backstreets, arrives at the gates as the sun slips under the evening. No crocuses now. A Carling can rolls across a ledger stone. He checks he's alone, kneels at the newest grave, logs the name in his pocketbook. He forces a hand through the grass seed then stands, dusts off his trousers, fingernails pulsing with clean dark earth.

He paces back along the yew-lined path, repeating his route in reverse. No cat on the wheelie bin. No bee at the window box. But a pigeon on the road with its breast to the clouds, the beginning of the rain, the rain driving slantways, the washing line, the wildflower bedsheets.

Blossom

Just past the tennis courts
at the gate to the memorial garden
I stop, pull out my sandwiches, sprawl
under the blossom tree –
        limbs arthritic
but so rich
it dresses me in petals and still
wraps pink around its shoulders.

I flick a ladybird off my sleeve.
She crouches in the dirt, breathing
for a moment, bracing her muscle
then hauls herself up to her feet
like you, rising from your armchair to make toast.

We came here for picnics
and you'd race me to the river,
we'd throw leftover brioche
for the goslings.
Spring after spring
we watched the water stain climb
half a brick higher
up the cottage garden wall.

First trip out with you
in your wheelchair (me clueless,
veering towards the reservoir), I left you
        under the knotted boughs
        dashed to the café for croissants;
when I came back
petals had collected in your lap.

Tidal Pool, Walpole Bay

The whole weekend is a tidal pool –
        grief lapping over but only a little,
gulls ringing around us, persistent

        as salesmen but we let them ring,
float on miracles – no shit in our hair
        and nothing to do except launch our bodies

onto one another's backs, yell *giddy-up!*
        flap in the water – sea-dogs and riders.
The North Sea tussles – huge

        bluish wrestler, in the gulp of a wave
last night's argument is gone.
        But we're unsinkable behind these walls.

Or is it the beach fires, the foil-baked
        bananas, the singing into beer cans
girl I didn't know you could get down like that.

        Those flame-lit faces are lighthouses.
Summer is melting into sea foam
        but it's easy not to care –

we smell the chip shop on the wind
        and all six of us turn,
front-crawl our way towards it.

This Picture of You in Trujillo

Seven capfuls of rum
        in your eyes, yeah you're backing

into the ocean, up to your hips,
        completely at ease.

Sometimes, we'd have nothing for breakfast
        and Fruit Loops for dinner.

Sundays drifted into Mondays,
        seamlessly as one sea

to the next. We flagged down trucks
        and weaved round warnings

of furious rock. Lakes of heat
        pooled on the concrete,

we sped straight through them.
        You climbed into a Jeep with a man

cradling a machete, and Cassie
        he clasped your hand.

Postcard from Palermo

Splayed on the bed of the studio apartment, lazy with heat
& hours of cheap wine. Blade of daylight has slipped the shutter
puncturing the dark, accents my kneecaps, pink satin scars.
Kids scuffling on Via del Celso, mopeds rioting over cobbles.
I'm picturing the view from the cathedral roof – pale brick palette
scrambling to the foothills, hills dropping deep into the Tyrrhenian Sea.
I'm picturing you (moonstone locket), touching up your blusher
for dinner with Olivia. Strip of sun on my skin's progressing,
gilding the hairs on my inner thigh. Months since we spoke –
wish you were here, to notice my body telling the time.

At the Pleasure Beach

I needed that day, it was a break in the rain –
we rode the Big Dipper, shared a plume of candyfloss,

laughed about nothing and lingered on South Pier
until the sky turned orange, then dark.

Sometimes thoughts go round in the wash,
come out while we sleep, tangled up

and coloured strange. Nights by the coast,
I dream I'm a cloud moving over the beach.

You're lazed on the sand, finishing the crossword.
I pour a few happy-sad raindrops on you,

you speak at the sky but your message is hushed
by a fracas of waves, the clatter of a rollercoaster

creeping to its peak. And the carriage feels
the pull of the drop but for a moment it holds,

towering over the Irish Sea
which seethes and settles, seethes and seethes.

Christ, I miss the mould

exploding   in the Kit-Kat mug
these days there's nothing worth
throwing dinner plates over
the drizzle just   exhausting
the toddler upstairs rides
her motorised truck
over solid wood flooring
I'm not even calling the council
the countertop screams the absence
    of toast crumbs
I'm making so much soup
I could cater a wedding
there's too much air   in this air
too few cig ends in the orchid
I'm weeping into my stockpot
for the neighbours to see
                as they stretch
to blow smoke out the back-
bedroom window   *look*
 wordless   muscular
   one lights a match
              for the other

Latrigg

A half mile higher we stop again
to look at a young silver birch sloped
sideways but caught, on its way to the ground,
in the crook of a neighbour's branches.
There's tenderness in that, the kind of comfort
you only get from spending the night
in a schoolfriend's bed. We pass the flask,
pour shots of coffee. You face south
towards Derwentwater, I look north
over Bassenthwaite. You tell me that you like it
when clouds sweep fast across the sky
as though they're late for a rehearsal

and I'm glad you've thought about that,
glad we're programmed to press on the world
all our surplus meanings. Like yesterday,
sizing up Latrigg from town, we noticed
that the pines formed immaculate flags
stamped across the hillside. Tonight, let's sit
outside the cemetery, name our constellations:
the argument, the question mark, the rocket ship.

Four Studies of Disappearing

After Maya Beano

⊹

The first time I came to the pink afternoon
I came here alone, my arms held low
like an angel testing her wings. Waist-deep
I wavered through the willowherb fields,
wanted to lose myself, to feel only
my fingers skimming the petals,
to see nothing but pink and deeper pink
and blue forever. I made three left turns,
found myself back at the thin dirt path.

⊹ ⊹

the next day I faded more quickly
each pace to the blue horizon
one sigh deeper away from my body
I felt lighter   I felt the willowherb
brushing my thighs   gentler   gentler
hardly at all   I couldn't tell which way
was home   tried to dream myself
towards it   fixed my eyes on the trees
on the spaces between the trees

⊹ ⊹ ⊹

you hung at the path
the pink seemed pinker
the willowherb deeper
than you'd imagined
focus on the trees I said
you said nothing
the rush of disappearing
washed my forearms pink
my cheeks flickered periwinkle

✤ ✤ ✤ ✤
fainter   fainter

          skin   pink petals

pink petals   skin

no need to breathe

air enters   stays

          willowherb   pink

sea rising to blue

horizon   ink-

          stain   ghost

Acknowledgements

Poems in this pamphlet have appeared in *Stand, Poetry Salzburg Review, Anthropocene* and on the websites of Poets & Players and the McLellan Poetry Competition.

I am grateful to everyone who has read and encouraged my work, especially Becky Varley-Winter, Pete Grogan, staff and students at the Manchester Writing School, writers at The Poetry Business writing days, and of course, all of the circus clowns and our eternal ringmaster John-Paul Burns.

A huge thank you to Aaron Kent and all at Broken Sleep Books.

I am grateful to the many teachers who have generously shared their time, knowledge, and love of poetry with me. Special thanks to Matt Carmichael, Andrew McMillian, and Ann and Peter Sansom.

Thanks to Jasper, for having the softest paws in the world always.

Endless love and gratitude to Liam and to my family. You are wonderful and I am so lucky.

LAY OUT YOUR UNREST

www.ingramcontent.com/pod-product-compliance
Lightning Source LLC
Chambersburg PA
CBHW051002030426
42339CB00007B/458